INDIA AS KNOWN TO THE ANCIENT WORLD

INDIA AS KNOWN TO THE ANCIENT WORLD

OR

INDIA'S INTERCOURSE IN ANCIENT TIMES WITH HER NEIGHBOURS, EGYPT, WESTERN ASIA, GREECE, ROME, CENTRAL ASIA, CHINA, FURTHER INDIA AND INDONESIA

BY

GAURANGANATH BANERJEE

GYAN

ISBN : 978-81-212-1531-2(HB)

First Published, 1921

Published, 2018

Published by

GYAN

Gyan Publishing House
5, Ansari Road
Daryaganj, New Delhi-110002
Phone: 011-47034999, 9811692060
www.gyanbooks.com
E-mail: books@gyanbooks.com

Printed at: G. Print Process, Delhi.

CONTENTS

PREFACE

The object of this little book is to offer a survey of the remarkable civilisation which arose in ancient India thousands of years ago and which influenced not only the manners, religion and customs of the people of the Malaya Archipelago and Indo-China, but gave also a thin veneer of culture to the nomads of Central Asiatic steppes, through her commercial enterprise and religious propaganda.

Now, civilisation is the outcome of reciprocal action and reaction : nations both giving and taking. Such a result is but to be expected when States come into contact with one another, when they acquire knowledge and intimacy of one another's institutions and are thus able to recognise and appreciate the merits of foreign organisations and perceive the defects of their own. In India, such reciprocal action and reaction we notice from the earliest times.

True it is that India has been periodically overrun by invaders both European and Asiatic ; nevertheless the transmission and assimilation of culture continues without a break. A conquering nation may carry its own civilization with it to the conquered. Culture is often forced upon the latter by measures coercive. The conquerors, on the other hand, may acquire culture from the vanquished ; or, without the subjection of a people, assimilation of culture may come about through the unconscious adoption of customs and modes of thought.

Throughout the earliest career of man in Central and Southern Asia, it is to India that we must turn as the dominant power by the sheer weight of its superior civilisation. To us, therefore who are the children of ancient India, it is of vital interest to lift the curtain and peer into the ages which bequeathed so precious a legacy to our forefathers. The moment seems opportune for grouping together the comparatively small amount of material at our disposal, with a view to presenting a general picture of India's intercourse with her neighbours at the dawn of history.

In this endeavour I have utilised the results of the researches of many *savants* and have added to them those of my own ; for the field of investigation is too large to be cultivated in its entirety by any single investigator. It has been my aim throughout to present only such results as may safely be regarded as certain and definite, and to abstain from those views which are fanciful or conjectural. I have moreover tried to tell the story without worrying the general reader with too many details.

To Dr. H. F. Helmolt's monumental work, the "*Weltgeschichte*" (published in English by Wm. Heinemann in London under the title "*The World's History*"), I am indebted, especially for India's relations with Indo-China and Malaya Peninsula. I also gratefully acknowledge my obligation to Dr. G. Hirth's invaluable book *The Ancient History of China* and to Sir S. Raffles' *History of Java*. To the colossal labours of Sir Gaston Maspero and Dr. Rappaport I have been indebted especially as regards Ancient Egyptian Trade with India. I also owe a debt to Mr. H. G. Rawlinson and Dr. Radha Kumud Mukherjee, forerunners in this particular branch of Indology.

Finally, I may say with Nicolaus Copernicus that "when I acknowledge that I shall treat of things in a very different manner from that adopted by my predecessors, I do so thanking them, for it is they who have opened up the roads which lead to the investigation of facts."

The University of Calcutta,
February, 1921

GAURANGANATH BANERJEE

"The history of trade is the history of the international commerce and of geography, and both combined form the history of the civilisation of our race".

O. Peschel.

WESTERN ASIA

The original home allotted to man by his Creator was in the mild and fertile regions of the East. There the human race began its career of improvement; and from the remains of Sciences which were anciently cultivated, as well as of Arts which were anciently exercised in India, we may conclude it to be one of the first countries in which men made any considerable progress in their early career. The wisdom of the "East" was celebrated in I. Kings and its productions were in request among the distant nations of antiquity (Gen. XXXVIII, 25). The intercourse between different countries was carried on at first entirely by land. Trade was carried on by means of caravans, particularly by nations who inhabited in the coast of the Arabian Sea, from the earliest period to which historical information reaches us. But notwithstanding every improvement that could be made in this manner of conveying the productions of the country to another by land, the inconveniences which attended it were obvious and unavoidable. Dark and serrated mountain ranges, glowing with heat and devoid of life, alternate with stretches of burning sand; sunken reefs and coral rocks near the shore; marauding bands of Bedouins infesting the caravan-routes; trade-jealousy and "preferential tariffs" of the myrmidons of custom-houses prevented or at least threw obstacles in the way of this mode of conducting commerce. So a method of communication more easy and expeditious was sought and the ingenuity of man gradually discovered that the rivers, the arms of the sea, and even the ocean itself were destined to open and facilitate intercourse with the various regions of the then known world. "Navigation and shipbuilding," observes Prof. Seignobos, "are arts so nice and complicated that they require the talents as well as the experience of many successive ages to bring them to any degree of perfection." From the raft or canoe, which first served to carry a savage over the rivulets which obstructed him in the chase, to the construction of a vessel capable of conveying a numerous crew or a considerable cargo of goods to a distant coast, is an immense stride. Many efforts would be made, many experiments would be tried and much labour as well as ingenuity would be employed before this arduous and important undertaking could be accomplished.

Even after some improvement was made in the art of shipbuilding, the intercourse of the nations with each other by sea was far from being extensive. From the accounts of the earliest historiographers, we learn that the navigation made its first efforts on the Mediterranean Sea and on the Persian Gulf. From an attentive inspection of the position of these two great inland seas, these accounts appear to be highly probable. These seas lay open the continents of Europe, Asia and Africa, and washing the shores of the most fertile and the most early civilised countries seemed to have been destined by Nature to facilitate their communication with one another. We find accordingly, that the first voyages of the Egyptians and the Phœnicians, the most ancient navigators mentioned in history, were made in the Mediterranean and the Red Sea. Their trade was not however long confined to the countries bordering upon these ; by acquiring early possession of the ports on the Arabian Sea, they extended the sphere of their commerce and are represented to have opened a communication by sea with India. Dr. Day asserts in his "History of Commerce," that "the beginnings of these sea-voyages are lost in the obscurity of the past. We know that they were highly developed by 1500 B. C., when Sidon was the leading city and that they did not cease to extend when the primacy of the Phœnician cities passed to Tyre. The Phœnicians taught the art of navigation to the ancient world ; their ships were long the accepted models of construction and the Greeks learned from them to direct their course at night by the North or, as the Greeks called it, the Phœnician Star."

But the question of the navigation on the Persian Gulf is still entirely shrouded in mist, as well as that of the Alpha and Omega of all early communications between the two countries—India and the land of Sumer and Akkad. It is inconceivable that the earliest civilisation of Chaldæa had not engaged in navigation on the "Sea of the East." At the period, when our knowledge begins however, we see this civilisation already withdrawing more northward, into the interior of the country. The most ancient inscriptions do not mention anything of such matters ;

and thus we must probably for a long time be content to leave the question unsolved. But incidentally we may notice that the great prosperity of the state called Elam and its obstinate and sturdy resistance first to Chaldæa, and then to the mighty Assyrian Empire may be partly explained by the wealth she acquired in trade with the countries on its eastern forntier ; for we know that Elam had a fleet manned with Phœnician crews in the great bay at the embouchure of the two streams, Tigris and Euphrates. Thus it is sufficient to make us recognise that Elam, in consequence of its position and civilisation, really was the connecting link between the civilised countries of Nearer and Farther Asia and the predecessor of the eastern half of the later Persian Empire. So if the trade with India and Western Asia is one of the most important factors in the history of the world, Elam must also in the days of its splendour have interfered, if unable to assist, in these trade-relations and always have had an important word in the matter. And if in the Persian time, under the full light of history, the Aramaic script wandered to India and farther eastward, such an event may equally well have happened in the earlier millennia. This fact is expressed less clearly, but still distinctly enough, in the recurrence of the Babylonian legend of the Flood among the Indians, to which many other points in common will some day be added (vide Ragozin, *Vedic India*).

Now, the principal sources of our knowledge, such as it is, of early Indian trade, are derived from scattered hints in the ancient authors of India, beginning with the Indian Scriptures and from several passages in the Mahabharata, notably the enumeration of gifts that were brought by the various nations to the great Rājasuya of Yudhistira.* As regards navigation in Vedic India, it was diligently pursued, which could not but be expected in a district so intersected by streams as that of the Indus; even voyages on the open sea are hinted at and merchants are mentioned, though seldom. Prof. Dr. Kaegi in his Introduction to the "Rig Veda" says that there was navigation in the streams of the Punjab and on the Ocean (cf. the Voyage of Prince Bhujya) and trade only existed in barter. And it is narrated there, that the two Aswins (who represent morning and evening twilight) brought back Prince Bhujya, who sailed in a hundred-oared ship ('Satâritram nawam') and went to sea and was nearly drowned, "in vessels of their own along the bed of the Ocean." Thus

> "Safe comes the ship to haven,
> Through billows and through gales;
> If once the great Twin brethern
> Sit shining on the sails."

But the first trade between the West and India of which we have any definite knowledge was that carried on by the Phœnician and Hebrew mariners from Ezion-Geber on the Red Sea; and an account we have of this trade implies, on the part of the Phœnicians, a previous acquaintance with the route. The Phœnicians first made their appearance on the Erythræan or the Red Sea, by which we must understand the whole Indian Ocean between Africa and the Malaya Peninsula; and curiously the Puranas thus represent

* For internal evidence, vide my article on "Peregrinations of the Ancient Hindus" in "Hindustan Review" May, 1918.

it, when they describe the waters of the Arunôdadhi, as reddened by the reflection of the solar rays from the southern side of the Mount Sumeru, which abounds with red rubies. Of the fact that a trade existed between Western Asia and Babylonia on the one hand and Hindusthan on the other, there cannot be any doubt. M. D'Anville suggests three routes for this intercourse with the Western World. The first climbs up the precipitous and zigzag passes of the Zagros Range, which the Greeks called the "Ladders", into the treeless regions of Persia. This route was barred for centuries by the inveterate hostility of the mountaineers and did not become practicable until "the Great King Darius" reduced the Kurdish highlanders to a condition of vassalage. The second traverses the mountains of Armenia to the Caspian Sea and Oxus and descends into India by the passes of the Hindukush. Articles of commerce doubtless passed along this way from very early times ; but the trade was of little importance, fitful, intermittent and passed through many intermediate hands, until the Parthian domination obliged more merchants to take this route.

Lastly, there is the Sea ; and this alone affords a direct and constant intercourse.

Now the question of main importance is at what period did regular maritime intercourse first arise between India and Western Asia ? From the history of the Chinese coinage, it is quite certain that an active sea-borne commerce sprang about 700 B. C. between Babylon and Farther East and that India had an active share in it. From the time of Darius Hystaspes (c. 500 B.C.) the Babylonians lost their monopoly in it and it passed largely into the hands of the Arabs, whom the Greeks found in possession. Ample evidence is forthcoming that maritime intercourse existed between India and Babylon in the seventh century B. C.

Firstly : Shalmaneser IV of Assyria (727-722 B. C.) received presents from Bactria and India, specially Bactrian camels and Indian elephants. (Dr. Winckler)

Secondly : Mr. H. Rassam found a beam of Indian cedar in the palace of Nebuchadrezzar III of the Neo-Babylonian Empire (c. 580 B. C.) at Birs Nimrud, part of which is now exhibited in the British Museum.

Thirdly : The Baveru Jātaka relates the adventures of certain Indian merchants, who took the first peacock by sea to Babylon. The Jātaka itself may go back to 400 B. C., but the folk-tales on which it is founded must be much older. Prof. Minayeff saw in the Baveru Jātaka the oldest trace in India of Phœnicio-Babylonian intercourse.

Fourthly : Certain Indian commodities were imported into Babylon even in the days of Solomon c. 900 B. C. and they were known to the Greeks and others under their Indian names. Rice, for instance, had always been a principal article of export from India (vide the Periplus of the Erythræan Sea) and it was a common article of food in the time of Sophocles (Gk. Oryza is identical with the Tamil, arisi or rice). Again Aristophanes repeatedly mentions peacock and assumes that it was well-known to his audience as the common-fowl with which he contrasts it. Peacocks, rice and Indian sandal-woods were known in Palestine under their Tamil names in the days of Hebrew chroniclers of Kings and Genesis.

Fifthly: Baudhāyana's condemnation of the Northern Aryans who took part in the sea-trade, proves that they were not the chief agents, though they had a considerable share in it.*

These evidences then warrant us in the belief that maritime commerce between India and Babylon flourished at least in the seventh and sixth centuries B. C. It was chiefly in the hands of the Dravidians, although the Aryans also had a share in it; and as Indian traders settled afterwards in Arabia (vide Lassen, Ind. Alter. ii, p. 580) and on the east coast of Africa, and as we find them settling at this very time on the coast of China, we cannot doubt that they had their settlements inBabylon also. "Crowds of strangers lived in Babylon," says Berossus (c. 350 B. C.). But the 7th and the 6th centuries are the culminating period of Babylonian greatness. Babylon which had been destroyed by Sennacherib, and rebuilt by Esarhaddon and later on beautified by Nebuchadrezzar III—Babylon, which owed her importance and her fame to the sanctity of her temples—now appears before us all of a sudden, as the greatest commercial entrepôt of the world. There was no limit to her resources and to her power. She arose and utterly overthrew her ancient rival and oppressor Nineveh. With Nebuchadrezzar she became the wonder of the world. No other city could rival her magnificence. Splendid in her battlements and streets, her temples and palaces and gardens, she glowed with resplendent colour under the azure sky, the acknowledged mistress of the nations, regally enthroned among the palm-groves on either bank of the broad swift-flowing flood of the Euphrates. The

* See Mr. J. Kennedy's learned article in J. R. A. S., 1898.

merchants of all countries made her their resort; the camels of Yemen and the mules of Media jostled each other in her streets. The secret of her greatness lay in her monopoly of the treasures of the East, in the shouting of the Chaldæans in their ships and in the swarthy Orientals who frequented her bazaars.

A commerce, frequent and direct, between the Semites of Mesopotamia and the Indians could be carried on only by the way of the sea. The overland routes were not impracticable, in fact the desert steppes of Asia formed the mercantile ocean of the ancients—the companies of camels, their fleets. The physical obstacles could be overcome, and practically the earliest trade between India and Mesopotamia crossed the lofty passes of the Hindukush and wound its perilous way along the banks of the Oxus. But the commerce was from hand to hand, and from tribe to tribe, fitful, rare and uncertain and never possessed any importance. Similarly, the normal trade-route from the Persian Gulf to India could never have been along the inhospitable deserts of Gedrosia. Doubtless then, more than one adventurous vessel reached India by hugging the shore prior to the seventh century B.C., although the records are lost and commercial results therefrom were negligible. But the exploring expeditions dispatched by Darius in 512 B. C. from the mouth of the Indus under Skylax of Karyanda and two centuries later by Alexander the Great, under Nearchos, the Admiral of the Macedonian Fleet, show the difficulties and dangers of this route, the time it occupied and the ignorance of the pilots. The clear-headed author of the Periplus, it is true, says that small ships made formerly voyages to India, coasting along the shore until Hippalus first ventured to cross the ocean by observing the monsoon. The monsoon was known however from the earliest times to all who sailed along the Arabian and African coast. Down to the very end of the Middle Ages, the voyage from Ormuzd to India was rarely attempted except at the commencement of the middle of the monsoon.

EGYPT

The trade of the ancient Egyptians had given them very little knowledge of geography. Indeed the whole trade of the Egyptians was carried on by buying goods from their nearest neighbours on one side and selling them to those on the other side of them. Long voyages were unknown; and though the trading-wealth of Egypt had mainly arisen from carrying the merchandise of India and Arabia Felix from the ports on the Red Sea to the ports on the Mediterranean, the Egyptians seem to have gained no knowledge of the countries from which these goods came. They bought them of the Arab traders who came to Cosseir and the Troglodytic Berenicê from the opposite coast; the Arabs had probably bought them from the caravans that had carried them across the desert from the Persian Gulf; because these land journeys across the desert were for the Arabs both easier and cheaper than a coasting voyage. On the contrary, India seems to have been known to the Greeks prior to Alexander, as a country which by sea was to be reached by way of the Euphrates and the

Persian Gulf; and though Skylax had dropped down the river Indus, coasted Arabia and then reached the Red Sea, this voyage was either forgotten or disbelieved, and in the time of the Ptolemies it seems probable that nobody thought that India could be reached by sea from Egypt. Arrian indeed thought that the difficulty of carrying water in their small ships with large crews of rowers, was alone great enough to stop a voyage of such a length along a desert-coast which could not supply them with fresh water.

The long voyages of Solomon and Necho had been limited to circumnavigating Africa; the voyage of Alexander the Great had been from the Indus to the Persian Gulf: hence it was that the court of Euergetes was startled by the strange news that the Arabian guards on the coast of the Red Sea, had found a man in a boat by himself, who could not speak Koptic, and whom they afterwards discovered to be an Indian who had sailed straight from India and had lost his ship-mates (c. 200 B.C.). He was willing to show any one the route by which he had sailed; and Eudoxus of Cyzicus in Asia Minor came to Alexandria to persuade Euergetes to give him the command of a vessel for this voyage of discovery. A vessel was given him; and though he was but badly fitted out, he reached a country, which he called India, by sea and brought back a cargo of spices and precious stones. He wrote an account of the coasts which he visited and it was made use of by Pliny. In the course of these attempts at maritime discovery and searchings for a cheaper means of obtaining the Indian products, the Greek sailors of Euergetes made a settlement in the island Dioscorides (now called Socotra) in the Indian Ocean and there met the trading vessels from India and Ceylon. This little island continued a Greek colony for upwards of seven centuries and Greek was the only language spoken there, till it fell under the Arabs, in the twilight of history, when all European possessions in Africa were overthrown. But the art of navigation was so far unknown that little use was made of this voyage of Eudoxus; the goods of India, which were all costly and of small weight, were, under the Ptolemies, still for the most part carried across the desert on camels' backs.

The maritime intercourse of Egypt with India in the epoch which immediately preceded the Roman rule, was not great and was carried on in the main by the Arabians. It was only through the Romans that Egypt obtained the great maritime traffic to the East. "Not 20 Egyptian vessels in the year," says a contemporary of Augustus, "ventured forth under the Ptolemies from the Arabian Gulf: now 120 merchantmen annually sail to India from the port of Myos Hormos alone." Alexandria, under the Romans became the great entrepôt of the trading world, not only having its own great trade in grain, but being the port through which the trade of India and Arabia passed to Europe, and at which the Syrian vessels touched on their way to Italy. The harbour was crowded with masts and strange prows and uncouth sails and the quays always were busy with loading and unloading; while in the streets might be seen men of all languages and all dresses, copper-coloured Egyptians, swarthy Jews, lively, bustling Greeks and haughty Italians, with Asiatics from neighbouring coasts of Syria and Cilicia and even dark Ethiopians, painted Arabs, Bactrians, Scythians, Persians, and Indians, all gay in their national costumes. Alexandria was a spot in which Europe met Asia and each wondered at the strangeness of the other.

It was not till the reign of Claudius (A. D. 41) that the route through Egypt to India became really known to the Europeans. The historian Pliny, who died in 79 A. D., has left us a contemporary account of these early voyages. "It will not be amiss," says Pliny, in his Natural History, "to set forth the whole of the route from Egypt, which has been stated to us of late, upon information on which reliance may be placed and is here published for the first time. The subject is one well worthy of our notice, seeing that in no year does India drain our Empire of less than 550 millions of sesterces* giving back her own wares in exchange, which are sold among us at fully one hundred times their cost price................ To those who are bound for India, Ocelis is the best place for embarkation. If the wind called Hippalus happens to be blowing, it is possible to arrive in 40 days, at the nearest mart in India called Muziris.† This however is not a desirable place for disembarkation, on account of the pirates which frequent its vicinity; nor in fact is it very rich in articles of merchandise. Besides the roadstead for shipping is at a considerable distance from the shore, and the cargoes have to be conveyed in boats, either for loading or for discharging." "At the moment I am writing these pages," continues Pliny, "the name of the king of the place is Cælobotras. Another

* About 80 lakhs of rupees.

† Modern Mangalore.

port and a much more convenient one, is that which lies in the territory of the people called Nelcyndi,—Baracê by name. Here king Pandion used to reign, dwelling at a considerable distance from the mart in the interior, at a city known as Modeira. Travellers set sail from India on their return to Egypt, at the beginning of the Egyptian month Tybus, which is our December; if they do this, they can go and return in the same year."

The places on the Indian coast, which the Egyptian merchant vessels then reached, are verified from the coins found there. A hoard of Roman gold coins has been dug up quite recently near Calicut, under the roots of a banyan tree. It had been buried by an Alexandrian merchant on his arrival from a voyage and left safe under the cover of the sacred tree to await his return from a second journey. But he died before his return and his secret died with him. The products of the Indian trade were chiefly silk, diamonds and other precious stones, ginger, spices and ivory.

To Pliny's survey we must add the valuable geographical knowledge given by the author of the Periplus of the Erythræan Sea, which has come down to us in an interesting document, wherein he mentions the several sea-ports and their distances, with the tribes and cities near the coast. The trade of Egypt to India and Arabia was then most valuable and carried on with great activity; but as the merchandise in each case was carried only for short distances from city to city, the merchants could gain but little knowledge of where it came from or of where it was going. Even under Justinian part of the Egyptian trade to the East was carried on through the islands of Ceylon and Socotra ; but it was chiefly in the hands of the uneducated Arabs, who were little able to communicate to the world much knowledge of the countries from which they brought their highly-valued goods. At Ceylon they met with traders from beyond the Ganges and China, from whom they bought the silk which the Europeans had formerly thought a product of Arabia.

That the Roman legions failed to make their way to India across the mountainous frontiers of Western Iran, following in the footsteps of Alexander, is a fact of vast historical importance. The civilisation of the Western world, which had once been borne by Alexander as far as the Indus, was destined for more than a thousand years to be cut off from all contact with the world of the East ; for the small flame of Greek culture that shed its feeble rays over Bactria counted for little and was soon extinguished. It is true that Greek art lived on in India for many years longer ; but it finally became absorbed and lost all resemblance to its former self in the hands of the Indians (vide my book "*Hellenism in Ancient India*"). It is also true that the teachings of Indian sages were echoed in the Western world of esoteric sects and schools of Philosophy, but the mutual labour of civilisation was completely broken off for the time.

GREECE AND ROME

As was to be expected, the earliest voyages and travels of the ancient Greeks, which have come down to us are enshrined in poetry and surrounded with a certain halo of fiction, though accepted as genuine history by the uncritical ancients. The first of the legends of Greece and anterior to Homer is the voyage of the Argonauts. It was developed, enlarged and localised by succeeding chroniclers. From Mimnermus, the oldest authority, we learn no further than that Æites lived on the banks of the ocean-stream in the farthest East, and Homer alludes to the voyage, as even in his time world-famous. But in this critical age, the only thing that can be conceded is that at a very remote period, some adventurous Greek navigators did penetrate through the straits of the Dardenelles and the Bosphorus into the Euxine. The geographical notions of Homer as gathered from his two great epics are embodied in the statements, namely that the Ethiopians, a burnt-faced people, lived in the south of Egypt, on the borders of the ocean-stream at the extreme limits of the world and that they were divided into two portions, the one dwelling towards the setting and the other towards the rising sun.

One of the first prose writings in the Greek language is the geographical treatise of Hecateus, which was probably published before the end of the sixth century B. C. The work was named Periodus, that is, Description of the Earth. Unfortunately it has perished and what we know of it, is collected from the fragments quoted in the works of later writers, which have been brought together and published by Müller-Didot in his *Fragmenta Historicum Græcorum.* Between Homer and Hecateus, there had been a great widening of the horizon. A long time after Hecateus, however, curiosity and love of enquiry seemed to have urged the travellers to visit foreign countries and among the earliest of this class was Pythagoras, who certainly visited Egypt about 500 B: C. Still everything beyond the basin of the Mediterranean was only known to the Greeks by the reports of other nations. No Greek navigator adventured beyond the Pillars of Hercules or found his way to the Erythræan Sea. Whatever rumours were current about Ethiopia or India must have reached the Greeks through the Egyptians, the Phœnicians, and later on the Persians. But the conquest of the Greek cities in Asia Minor by the generals of the great Persian monarchs had let in a new flood of light; the Milesians and the Samians became subjects of a monarch who resided in Mesopotamia and this must have opened to the conquered a new and wonderful world. Darius conducted an expedition against the Scythians crossing into Europe. Soon began the Persian wars and the Greek citizens became aware of the kingdoms and cities, of races and languages, of which Homer had never dreamt. It must be admitted however that from Hecateus the Greeks had already heard the names of the Caspian Sea, of India and the river Indus, as also of the Persian Gulf.*

Next come the monumental works of Herodotus. His works have survived to our times and form an epoch in geography as well as in history. Proceeding southward it appears clearly that his knowledge was confined to the limits of the Persian kingdom. Of Arabia he had only a vague knowledge, but the navigation on the Red Sea was established and commerce supplied not only the frankincense and myrrh of Arabia Felix, but cinnamon and cassia of a country

* Vide Cust, *The Geography of the Greeks and the Romans.*

far beyond India or Ceylon. He alludes to tides as a phenomenon, with which the Greeks were not familiar in their own inland sea. To Herodotus we are indebted for all we know about the voyage of Skylax from the mouths of the Indus to the Persian Gulf; from him we first hear of the cotton and the bamboos of India and of the famous story of the gold-digging ants as large as foxes and many wonderful myths about India.

The founding of Alexander's Empire brought to the East an expansion of Greek culture; it promoted an exchange of commodities between East and West, and a mixture of "Barbarian" and Greek nationalities, such as the ancient world had never seen before. Iberian tribes in Spain, Celtic clans in Southern France, Etruscan towns, Italian arts and crafts, Egyptian legends and Assyrian military systems, Lycian sepulchral architecture and Carian monuments, the works of Scythian goldsmiths and Persian palaces, had already long been subject to Greek influence; so that the Greeks won their place in the history of the world far more as citizens of the Mediterranean sphere than by their domestic struggles. The founding of Alexandria and revival of Babylon had created great cities in the East, which from the height of their intellectual and material civilisation, were destined to be the centres of the new Empire. The long stored-up treasures of the Achæmenids once more circulated in the markets; the observations and calculations of the Chaldæan astronomers, which went back thousands of years, and the unrivalled philosophical doctrines of the Vedanta and Upanishads became available to the Greeks. Alexander thought that the political organisation of Hellenism, the world-empire, was only possible by a fusion of races. But the nuptials of the Orient and the Occident, which were celebrated at the wedding festival in Susa, remained a slave-marriage, in which the West was the lord and master. By the transplantation of nations from Asia to Europe and from Europe to Asia, it was proposed to gain for the world-monarchy, with its halo of religious sanctity, the support of those disconnected masses which were united with the ruling dynasty alone, but had no coherence among themselves. Thus the old hereditary culture of the East and the new-born energy of the West seemed to be welded together and Greek had become the language of the civilized provinces of the Western Asia. And this inheritance of Alexander was not transitory. Even if on that summer's evening of June 13, 323 B. C., when the news that he was dead and that the world was without a master burst on the passionately excited populace at Babylon, the plans for the future were abandoned and the disintegration of the mighty empire was inevitable, yet the creation of a new sphere of culture, which partially embraced the ancient East, was the work of Alexander.

The focus of political activity shifted towards the East and the direction of the world-commerce changed ; the centres were now the Greek cities founded or revived by Alexander. The combined commerce of Ethiopia, India, Arabia and Egypt itself, converged on Alexandria, that city of world-trade and cosmopolitan civilisation. Seleucia on the Tigris, not Babylon, became the metropolis of the fertile plains of

Mesopotamia. Thus even the remote countries of the East now drew nearer to Hellenism. The Greeks of Asia Minor had of course belonged to the same empire as a part of the Indian nation, so that commerce was early able to bring into the Punjab the products of Greek art ; and philosophical ideas such as the Indian doctrine of the transmigration of souls found their way to Greek territory. It is certain that the Indians had become familiar with the Greek alphabet at the time of the grammarian Panini, about 4th century B. C., but it was not until Alexander's expedition, that the Indian trade, which was now so important to Alexandria, became a part of Greek commerce. The Indian custom of ornamenting golden vessels with precious stones was adopted in the sphere of Greek culture ; and Indian jacinth became a favourite material with lapidaries. With the Indian precious stones came their names, opal, beryl, etc. into the West. Indian fables influenced the Greek travellers' tales and the Greeks welcomed the fantasies of the Indian folklore. In the age subsequent to Alexander, a flourishing commerce was maintained with India and Megasthenes in astonishment tells us of the marvellous country—its splendid mountains and groves, its smiling, well-watered plains and the strong, proud race of men who breathe the pure air.

But an influence also spread from the West to the East. A typical instance of this is shown by the fact that the Indian expressions connected with warfare (*e.g.* Kalinos, a horse-bit = Sans. Khalina ; Surigê, a subterranean passage = Sans. Suranga) found their way from Greek into Sanskrit. The plastic arts were enriched. Doric (Kashmere), Ionic (Taxila) and Corinthian (Gândhâra) pillars arose in that fairy land and the symbol of God of Love, the dolphin, may have been transported from Greece to India by the sculptor's art.* The relations of Asoka with the West in the field of religion and politics are stated in his XIIIth inscription, in which is mentioned that the "Pious" king had succeeded in winning over even the Greek princes, Amtiyoga (Antiochus), Tulumaya (Ptolemaus), Amtikina (Antigonus), Magas of Cyrene and Alikasadala (Alexander of Epirus). Greek vitality must have been latent in these kingdoms of Greek *conquistadores*, since they did not shrink from the danger of mutual hostility. But their importance for the establishment of relations between Greek speaking world, India and East Asia had not yet been sufficiently appreciated. King Demetrius (180-165) and the town of Demetrias (Dattamittiyaka-Yonaka) which he built, appear in the stirring verses of the Mahâbhârata. Tibetan hordes drove him out of Bactria and forced him completely into the Punjab. The huge gold coins of his successor Eukratides, with the bust of a king and a horseman (Dioscuros) are described by Chinese records of the first century B.C. Indian culture and philosophy must have gained a footing in Bactrian kingdom by degrees. King Menander (c. 125-95 B. C.) was already a Buddhist; but even when fading away, this Greek civilisation had strength enough to influence the adjoining Indo-

* For a detailed study of the Hellenic influence on the civilisation of ancient India, vide my book "Hellenism in Ancient India," (published by Messrs. Butterworth & Co., London and Calcutta).

Scythian territory, as is evidenced by the use of Greek letters and inscriptions on the coins of this empire.

Thus in the remotest east of the countries which were included in the habitable region on the fringe of the East Asiatic world, the Greek spirit wantonly prodigal of its forces, was tearing itself to pieces, yet nevertheless was able to influence coinage, art and astronomy, as far as India. In the Nile valley and at Babylon native authors such as Manetho and Berossus wrote in Greek ; and the Greeks explored the Red Sea, the Caspian, the Nile and the Scythian steppes. The same Hellenism had founded for itself in the West a province of Hellenic manners and customs and had completely enslaved it. This was the Roman Empire, now coming to the fore, which as it took its part in the international commerce, offered the Greek intellect a new home with fresh constitutional and legal principles.

In the first centuries before and after Christ, when the Kushanas were establishing themselves among the ruins of the Bactrian and other semi-Greek principalities of North-Western India, great changes were taking place in the West. Rome was absorbing the remains of the Empire of Alexander. Syria had already fallen and Egypt became a Roman province in 30 B. C. The dissensions of Civil War ended at Actium, after which Augustus settled down to organise and regulate his vast possessions. The effect of the Pax Romana upon trade was of course very marked. Piracy was put down, trade-routes secured and the fashionable world of Rome, undistracted by conflict, began to demand on an unprecedented scale oriental luxuries of every kind. Silk from China, fine muslins from India and jewels and pearls from the Persian coast were exported from eastern parts for personal adornment. Drugs, spices, condiments and cosmetics from the East fetched high prices in the bazars of Rome.

The news of the accession of Augustus quickly reached India. Many Indian states sent embassies to congratulate him, an honour never paid before to any Western prince. The most striking of these was one sent by an important king called, according to Strabo, Pandion. Prof. Rawlinson identifies him with Kadphises I. Strabo relates that Nicolaus Damascenus met at Antioch, Epidaphne the survivor of this Embassy to Augustus bearing a letter in Greek from the Indian prince. With them was Zarmanochegus (Sramanâchâryya) of Barygaza or Broach, who was evidently a Buddhist monk and who imitated Kalanos by burning himself on a funeral pyre at Athens. Allusions to this Embassy are made by Horace in his Odes. Florus and Suetonius refer to it and Dio Cassius speaks of its reception at Samos, B. C. 22-20 and mentions Zarmanos as accompanying it. It is also mentioned by Hieronymus in his translation of the Canon Chronicon of Eusebius, but is placed by him in the 3rd year of the 188th Olympiad *i.e.* 26 B. C.* Indian Embassies visited Rome henceforward from time to time; as for instance, an embassy was sent in 41 A. D. from Ceylon to Emperor Claudius. Pliny relates of this Embassy that a freedman of Annius Plocamus, being driven into Hippuros, hearing about

---

* Vide Reinaud, *Relations politiques et commerciales de l' Empire Romain avec l'Asie Orientale*, and H. G. Rawlinson, *India and the Western World*, *loc. cit.*

Rome, sent thither Rachias and three other Ambassadors, from whom Pliny obtained the information about Ceylon embodied in his Natural History. It probably left Ceylon in the reign of Chandramukhasiva (41-52 A. D.). Another Indian Embassy came to Emperor Trajan about 107 A. D. and is said to have been present at the shows given by him to the Roman people. The fourth Embassy was sent to Antoninus Pius about 138 A. D. According to Reinaud, towards the middle of the 1st century A. D., Taxila is said to have been visited by Apollonius of Tyana. He reached India after traversing Khorasan, the Hindukush and the kingdom of Kabul. Apollonius was a philosopher of the School of Pythagoras and sought like that sage to extend his knowledge by travelling into foreign countries. He came to Hindusthan to explore the wonders of India and to make himself acquainted with the learning and wisdom of the Brahmans, the fame of whom had been spread in the West by the companions of Alexander the Great.

Trade between India and Rome continued to thrive steadily during the second and third centuries A. D. This was chiefly due to the discovery of the existence of the monsoon winds blowing regularly across the Indian Ocean by a captain of the name of Hippalus. To the Arab sailors the phenomenon was however no secret, as the term Monsoon from the Arabic Mauzim implies. There was a temporary lull in the demand of luxuries, after the extraordinary outburst of extravagance which culminated in the reign of Nero, but this did not have a serious effect upon commerce. Roman Emperors took an increasing interest in the Eastern questions, but we can only approximately determine how far the direct maritime traffic went towards the East. In the first instance, it took the direction of Barygaza (Broach), which great mart must have remained throughout the whole period the centre of the Egypto-Indian traffic. In the Flavian period, the whole West coast of India was opened up to the Roman merchants, as far down as the coast of Malabar, the home of the highly-esteemed and dearly-priced pepper, for the sake of which they visited the ports of Muziris (probably Mangalore) and Nelcynda (in Sanskrit, doubtless Nilkantha). Somewhat further to the south, in Cannanore, numerous Roman gold coins of the Julio-Claudian epoch have been discovered, which were formerly exchanged against the spices destined for the Roman kitchens. Thus the Western coast of India and even the mouth of the Ganges, to say nothing of the further Indian Peninsula, maintained regular commercial intercourse with the Roman Empire. Chinese silk was already at an early period sold regularly to the Occidentals, as it would appear, exclusively by the land-route and through the medium partly of the Indians of Barygaza, but chiefly of the Parthians.

That the Hindus did not always wait for others to come to them for goods is in evidence in a variety of ways. There is first the statement of Cornelios Nepos, who says that Q. Metellus Celer received from the king of the Suevi some Indians, who had been driven by storm into Germany in the course of a voyage of commerce (*vide* M'Crindle, Ancient India, p. 110). This is quite a precise fact, and is borne out by a number of tales of the voyages with the horrors attending navigation depicted in the liveliest colours in certain classes of writings both in Sanskrit and Tamil. So during this period and for a long time after, the Hindusthan proper kept touch with the outer world by way of land mainly ; while the Deccan kept itself in contact with the rest of the world chiefly by way of the sea. The Baveru Jātaka is certain proof of this intercourse by way of the sea. Still more remarkable is the fact that the ancient Hindu mariners used to have light-houses to warn ships and one such is described at the great port at the mouth of the Kavery, a big tower or a big palmyra trunk carrying on the top of it a huge oil-lamp.

Now, one of the most curious relics of the trade between Egypt and India during the Roman period, has been recently unearthed at Oxyrrhyncus. It is a papyrus containing a Greek farce of the second century A. D. which deals with the story of a Greek lady named Charition, who had been shipwrecked on the Canarese coast. The locality is identified by the fact that the king of the country addresses his retinue as *indon promoi*. Dr. Hultzsch is of opinion that the barbarous jargon in which they addressed one another is actually Canarese.

Again, Dio Chrysostom, who lived in the reign of Trajan, mentions Indians among the cosmopolitan crowds to be found in the bazars of Alexandria ; and he says that they came "by way of trade." Chrysostom's information about India, however, is not very accurate or striking. Much more accurate is the knowledge possessed by the Christian writer Clement of Alexandria, who died about 220 A. D. The most important of his statements are that the Brahmans despise death and set no value on life, because they believe in transmigration of souls and that the Semnoi (Buddhist Sramanas) worship a kind of pyramid, beneath which they imagine that the bones of a divinity of some kind lie buried. This remarkable allusion to the Buddhist Stupa is the earliest reference in Western literature to that unique feature of Buddhism and must have been derived from some informant intimately acquainted with the doctrines of Gautama Buddha. Clement distinguishes clearly between Sramanai and Brachmanai, while earlier writers like Megasthenes confuse them. Archelaus of Carrha (278 A. D.) and St. Jerome both mention Buddha by name and Buddha's story was narrated in the 8th century by John of Damascus as the life of a Christian Saint. We may notice incidentally here that Buddha has been canonised by the Christian Church under the appellation of St. Josaphat and has been included in the Martyrology of Pope Gregory XIII. In both the Roman and the Greek Churches, a day is set apart for St. Josaphat, which name is a corruption of Bodhisattwa. There is also reason to suppose that the story of the life of St. Eustathius Placidus is a version of Nigrodhamiga Jātaka. The influence of Buddhism on Christianity is still deeper. The more one reads of Pali Scriptures, the more one is convinced that the life and teachings of the Buddha, have been duplicated in the Gospels of the Apostles. The marvels and the wonders, which happened at the time of the Buddha's conception, birth, renunciation, temptation and enlightenment and which are to be found in the Achariya Abhuta Sutta, and Majjhima Nikaya, have a curious similarity to the miracles in the Gospels. It seems evident that Buddhism by means of its convents for monks and nuns, its legends of Saints, its worship of relics, and above all, through its rich ritual and hierarchical pomp did exercise an influence on the development of Christian worship and ceremony. We may therefore say with Prof. Sylvain Lèvi, that "it looks as if the whole universe moved under a common impulse to a work of salvation under the auspices of Buddhism."

With Cosmas Indicopleustes however, who visited India in the 6th century A. D., the last voyage of the ancient world was undertaken. The long night of the Middle Ages was now settling down upon the Western world. The Neo-Sassanian Empire, with its great Persian renaissance, had manned a fleet which was fast sweeping the Roman vessels from Eastern waters. In 364 A. D., the first fatal step in the downfall of Rome had been taken when the Empire was divided; in 410, came the Goths and Vandals and 50 years later the mightiest kingdom the world has ever seen had ceased to exist. Trade with the East, in spite of Persian rivalry struggled feebly on and the latest recorded Eastern Embassy to Constantinople reached that city in 530 A. D.

Mr. Sewell, who has made an elaborate study of the Roman Coins found in India, considers that an examination of the coin-finds leads to the following conclusions (*vide* J. R. A. S. 1904, p. 591):

(*i*) There was hardly any commerce between Rome and India during the Consulate.

(*ii*) With Augustus began an intercourse which, enabling the Romans to obtain Oriental luxuries during the early days of the

Empire, culminated in the time of Nero, who died A. D. 68.

(*iii*) From this time forward the trade declined till the time of Caracalla, A. D. 217.

(*iv*) From the time of Caracalla it almost entirely ceased.

(*v*) The maritime activity revived again, though slightly, under the Byzantine Emperors.

He also infers that the trade under the early Emperors was chiefly in luxuries ; under the later ones in industrial products ; and under the Byzantines the commerce was with the South-West of India and not with the interior. He moreover differs from those who find an explanation of this fluctuation in the political and social condition of India itself, and the facilities or their absence for navigating the seas ; and considers that the cause is to be sought for in the political and social condition of the Romans themselves. We fully agree with this view of Mr. Sewell as is borne out by the contemporary history of Rome about the 4th and 5th centuries A. D.

CENTRAL ASIA

Till comparatively recent times, the vast highlands of Asia with their glittering ramparts of eternal snow, their pasture grounds, their bleak deserts and verdant oases, were regarded with awe by the civilised nations. It seems that science in harmony with the religions and myths of so many people has succeeded in demonstrating by almost irrefragable proofs that Central Asia was the primitive home of mankind, the cradle, whence our own forefathers were sent out in the pride of youth to find out eventually a new home in Europe, while others descended into India. The mass of nebulous tradition is brought into contact with the traces of widely diverse nationalities and religions and must consult in its turn the annals of the Indians, Iranians, Greeks, Scythians, Chinese, Turks and Russians. Indeed the earliest references to Turkestan that have reached us, are contained in the Indian and Iranian Epics and lend colour to the theory that the Pamirs were the birth-place of the Aryan race.* Thus the belief in the importance of Central Asia for the earliest history of mankind was not altogether irrational. Around this citadel of the world lay, clustered in wide semicircle, the ancient countries of civilisation, Babylonia, China and India, and all who believe in a common fountain-head of these higher civilisations must look for it in Central Asia. In later times, the importance of Middle Asia for the history of mankind seems indeed much changed but not less perceptible. It no longer produces the germs of civilisation, but like an ever-glowing volcano, sends out streams of warlike nomads and shakes the earth far and wide, so that smiling lands become desolate and prosperous towns sink into dust. From the earliest times to the present day mankind has been deeply influenced by the existence of Central Asia and its races. India was repeatedly overrun by hordes of Central Asiatic nomads, but for a long time it exercised little in-

---

* Vide Ch. de Ujfalvy, *Les Aryens au nord et au sud de l' Hindou Kouch.*

fluence generally on the steppe region and almost none politically, since the barrier of the Himalayas was a deterrent from military enterprises and apart from this, the natural features of Tibet offered no attraction to a conqueror. But here, as in so many other cases, the spirit of religion has been mightier than the sword. Northern India, that great seminary of religious and philosophic thought, gradually made its influence felt in Central Asia and by Buddhist propaganda revolutionised the lives and opinions of the nomads. It was of course a case of scattered seeds, which were carried across the mountains and struck root independently, and we must not imagine any permanent union of Indian Philosophy with the nomad culture of the steppes.

The civilised countries of Western Asia were better protected than India against the tide of restless nomads. Between the Caspian Sea and the Himalayas rise the mountains of Khorassan and Afghanistan. Eastward of these, the fertile districts of the Oxus and the Jaxartes, where agricultural colonies and fortified towns could grow up, formed a vanguard of civilisation. Between the Caspian and the Black Sea, the Caucasus rises like a bulwark built for the purpose and cuts off Western Asia from steppes of Southern Russia, that ancient arena of nomad hordes. So long as the natural boundaries are maintained, the fertile plains of Western Asia were safe from the raids and invasions of the nomads. But the people of Iran, who guarded civilisation there, at length succumbed to the attack. The nomads found homes to their liking in the steppes, which abound in Iran, Syria and Asia Minor and consequently preserved their individuality far longer than in China and were only partially absorbed by the peoples they had conquered. Europe on the other hand was never able to ward off the inroads made from Central Asia. The Huns advanced to the Atlantic, the Avars and Hungarians invaded France, the Mongols reached Eastern Germany and the Osman wave spent itself against the walls of Vienna. That continent still harbours in the Magyars, the Turks and numerous Finnish and Mongolian tribes, the remnants of these inhabitants of the Heart of Asia.

A prolonged study of the historical traditions, which delight in recording the wars, murders and ravages of these nomads, and which picture the absolute terror which the incursions of these roving Asiatic tribes filled the hearts of the survivors, might well lead us to paint the perpetrators of such horrors in the darkest colours and to consider them as a species of ravenous wild beasts rather than as beings deserving the name of men. But such a view would be premature. The nature of herdsman, who grows up on the wild steppe and in consequence of his wanderings is forced to limit his possessions to a few movables, has a simplicity which is not devoid of dignity. The wide, clear horizon of his home is reflected in his temperament. The flowers of imagination and thought, which blossom so magnificently in the tropical plains of India or in the luxuriant gardens of Iran, find no nourishment in the wild steppes of Central Asia. A sober clearness of thought is as characteristic of the inhabitants of Middle Asia, as of the Arabs who grow up on a similar soil.

The period of more certain history, which begins

with the founding of the Bactrian Empire, shows us that India, which from all time had possessed a magic attraction for every conquering people was one of their first victims. But the southern part of the Bactrian Empire stood a bulwark against their inroads for some hundred years more. Then about 25 B. C. Kujula Kadphises, who had reunited Yue-Chi after their division into five clans, subdued the modern Afghanistan. This immediately opened the road to the Indian possessions of the Bactrian Empire. About the year 10 A.D., his successor Huomo Kadphises advanced into North-Western India and thus laid the foundation of the Indo-Scythian Empire. Undeniably the fact that Bactria as far as the borders of Central Asia was then united with large portions of India under one rule, did much to make the Indian influence, especially Buddhism then flourishing in India, felt far away northward. India generally entered into closer and more direct relations with Central Asia. Fifty years after the establishment of the Indo-Scythian Empire, the Buddhist propaganda had already reached China.

But while a large part of Central Asia first acquires importance for the history and culture of mankind on the appearance of nomad peoples and as the fountain-head of a disintegrating force, the Tarim basin, which is also called Eastern Turkestan or High Tartary, claims the attention of the historian far earlier and in another sense. The Tarim basin formed in ancient days the bridge between the Eastern and Western Asiatic civilisation, even if it was not an international highway, and witnessed a higher civilisation develop in its fertile regions. The key to many problems of the pre-historic period lies buried under the burning sands of Eastern Turkestan.

The ancient trade-communications through the Tarim basin are certainly to be regarded as a relic of the former connection with civilisation. The nomads, however as such, are not inclined to amass the heavy goods, which the town merchants store up in their vaults. In the Tarim basin, therefore, the real traders were always to be found among the settled inhabitants of the oases, although the security and success of their commerce depended on the good-will of the nomads. [The earliest recorded trade which passed through the Tarim basin and brought Eastern and Western Asia in some sort of communication was the silk-trade]. Obstacles indeed were presented by the great extent of the province, the peculiarities of its geography and soil, the vast deserts which intersected it and the lawless hordes which infested it. As it was impossible for a single traveller to undertake these long and arduous journeys it became necessary to collect companies either sufficiently numerous to defend themselves or able to pay for their protection of a body of guards. Such bodies of men or *Caravans* as we call them, could not be collected at a moment's notice or in every place; and it was necessary that a rendezvous should be appointed, so that the merchants and travellers might know where to join a sufficient force for their common defence. In like manner, the places of resort for the sale as well as the purchase of their merchandise were necessarily fixed, being recommended by their favourable position or by some other circumstance, such as long usage. In the vast steppes and sandy deserts, which they had to traverse, Nature had sparingly allotted to the travellers a few scattered places of rest. Such places of rest became also entrepôts of commerce and not infrequently the sites of temples and sanctuaries, under the protection of which the merchant prosecuted his trade, and to which pilgrims resorted ; and these centres frequently grew to great and opulent cities and contributed by motives of interest or necessity to attract to the same route the various bands of travellers, e. g., Samarkand, Kashgar, Khotan &c.

The towns and trading settlements in the Tarim basin, which are mentioned by Aristeas, can partially be identified with still existing modern localities. This is impossible in case of many, as may be concluded by the great number of towns buried beneath the sands which have been recently explored by Dr. Sven Hedin and Sir M. A. Stein. Further aid towards identification are furnished by the accounts of the Macedonian merchant Maes or Titianus, who enables us to fix the stations on the East Asiatic trade-route in the first century A.D. This road led from Samarkand to Ferghana, whence the "Stone Tower" and the valley of the Kisil Su were reached, at the entrance of which an important trading-town lay in the territory of Kasia. This was certainly the modern Kashgar, for which natural advantages of situation have secured uninterruptedly since ancient times a foremost position among the cities of the Tarim basin. But the connection with India, the beginnings of which are obscure, was of great importance to this civilisation. In this way, Eastern Turkestan became the bridge on which Indian manners and customs and above all Indian religion passed both to China and the rest of Central Asia, destined in course of time to work great revolutions in the character and habits of the Central Asiatic peoples.

No success, it is true, attended the attempts to come into direct communication with India through Tibet, and thus obviate the necessity of bringing Indian goods by a detour through the Tarim basin, although the Emperor Wu Ti made various efforts with this object in view and a small transit trade directly from India to Tibet must have been in existence long before his time. Maritime trade flourished at a later time, when the distance between the Chinese and Indian ports had been immensely lessened by the conquest of Southern China. It is significant that the real impetus to maritime commerce was not given until the second century A.D. when the Chinese lost the command of the highways of Central Asia. The long series of disorders, which soon afterwards broke out in China, completely checked any vigorous foreign policy, while the growing prosperity of the maritime commerce diminished to a great extent the importance of the overland trade. The petty states of the Tarim basin for many years subsequently led a quiet existence, more influenced by India than by China.

The importance of Buddhism for the west of Central Asia was chiefly felt before the Mongol period. The activity of the Buddhist missionaries outside the confines of India could not be vigorously exerted until the new religion had taken firm root in its native country. The period of the great Asoka marks both the victory of Buddhism in Northern India and the extension of political and religious influences towards the northwest. Kashmir, the bridge of Central Asia, recognised the suzerainty of Asoka. Even if Buddhism was unable to gain a firm footing there, still access had been obtained to the civilised oases of the Tarim basin, where the new religion quickly found a ready acceptance. In externals, this Buddhism, it must be admitted, was no result of purely Indian culture. In the first place, the Iranians had encroached upon India and left traces of their nationality on the manners and customs of the people ; and after the age of Alexander the Great, an offshoot of Hellenistic civilisation existed in Bactria which exercised an effective influence on the art and culture both in the Tarim basin and in north-western India. The Græco-Buddhist art and culture of northwest India found a new home in the Tarim basin. But generally speaking, Indians of pure race preached the new faith and their labours led naturally enough to a wide diffusion of Indian literature and culture. A large non-religious immigration also took place.

The influence of India apparently first made itself felt in Khotan, where a son of Asoka was said to have founded a dynasty. Khotan, owing to its geographical position, generally forms the connecting link between Central Asia and India and shows in its civilisation abundant traces of Indian influence (vide M. A. Stein, *The Sand-buried Ruins of Khotan.*) A large number of Buddhist shrines and monasteries were to be found in Khotan. The densely populated oasis. helped by its religious importance, repeatedly obtained great power, although it could not permanently keep it, since, as the key to the trade-route from India and as the southern road from the West to the East, it appeared a valuable prize to all the conquering tribes of Central Asia. From Khotan, Buddhism spread farther over the Tarim basin and its northern boundary. The clearest proof of this is to be found in the numerous cave-temples constructed on Indian model, as well as in the products of Græco-Buddhist art, which the explorations of Sir Marc Aurel Stein have brought to light, especially in the western part of Eastern Turkestan. It was certainly the settled portions of the nation, which were steeped in the ancient civilisation, that most eagerly adopted the higher forms of religion. The nomads were less satisfied with it. But the efforts of civilisation and religion to tame the barbarous people of Central Asia had been continued for many centuries. Temples of Buddha, Zoroastrian seats of culture, Christian churches and Moslem mosques arose in the oases; industries flourished, trade brought foreign merchants into the country and those who aimed at a refinement of manners and customs and a nobler standard of life were amply provided with brilliant models. Of the nomads a less favourable account must be given; and yet in many of them the higher forms of religion had struck root. Skilled writers were to be found among them, and the allurements of civilised life made considerable impression. The road which was destined to lead these tribes out of their ancient barbarism had already been often trodden: the forces of civilisation seemed pressing on victoriously in every direction. The nomad spirit then once more rallied itself to strike a blow more formidable than any which had previously fallen. The effort was successful and, as the result of it, a region once prosperous and progressive lay for generations at the mercy of races whose guiding instincts were the joy of battle and the lust of pillage. The world glowed with a blood-red light in the Mongol age. Twice, first under Genghis Khan and his immediate successors and secondly under Timur, the hordes of horsemen burst over the civilised countries of Asia and Europe; twice they swept on like a storm-cloud, as if they wished to crush every country and convert it into a pasture for their flocks. And so thoroughly was the work of ravage and murder done, that to the present day, desolate tracts show the traces of their destructive fury. These were the last great eruptions of the Central Asiatic volcano before Civilisation ultimately triumphed.

CHINA

China is the only kingdom on the habitable globe, which has continued without interruption from a remote antiquity to modern times. Though later in date than Egypt and the kingdoms of Western Asia, yet its authentic history embraces a period of two thousand and five hundred years, while the comparatively high state of civilisation evidenced at the beginning of this epoch implies another one thousand and five hundred years of previous development. Remoteness and inaccessibility have invested this country, which was to East Asia what Greece and Rome were to Europe, with a mysterious splendour which has often led the investigators to misestimate its actual condition.

The Chinese literature, so vast in extent, contains very considerable accounts of the geography of Asia at different times and of the nations who lived in that part of the ancient world. The greater part of these accounts is to be found in the histories of the various dynasties which have up to the present time, successively ruled in China. At the end of each of these dynastic histories, twenty-four in number, a section more or less extensive is to be found devoted to the foreign countries and nations who came in contact with the Chinese Empire. They are generally termed *Sz' Yi*, the four kinds of barbarians, in allusion to the four quarters of the globe. These notions were probably collected by Chinese envoys, or compiled from the reports of the envoys or merchants of these countries coming to China. Almost all Chinese works treating of foreign countries drew their accounts from these sources ; and even the celebrated Chinese geographer, Ma Tuan Lin, who wrote under the Mongol dynasty, has for the greater part compiled his excellent work, the *Wen hien Thung Kao*, from the dynastic histories.* Another category of Chinese accounts of foreign countries are those drawn up in the form of narratives of journeys undertaken by the Chinese. It seems that the Chinese never travelled for pleasure or visited distant countries for the purpose of enlarging the sphere of their ideas. All the narratives of their travels owe their origin either to military expeditions or to official missions of the Chinese

* Vide Marquis d'Hervey de St. Denys, *Ethnographie des Peuples étrangers a la Chine.*

Emperors, or they are written by Buddhist and other pilgrims, who visited India or other parts of Asia in search of sacred literature. They often contain very valuable accounts regarding the ancient geography of Asia, but it is not easy to lay them under contribution in elucidating this subject in a scientific sense. Generally, it is very difficult to search them out, for they do not exist for the greater part as separate publications, but lie concealed among the numerous volumes of the Chinese collections of reprints (*ts'ung shu*). Many of these interesting ancient narratives are lost and their existence in former times is only known from ancient catalogues or by quotations of other Chinese authors.

Now, the Chinese records tell us that foreign trade in China had for a long time been covered by the name inseparable from the early foreign enterprises of the Chinese Courts, of "tribute." The word "tribute" in Chinese annals was nothing but a substitute for what might as well have been called "exchange of produce" or trade—the trade with the foreign nations being a monopoly of the Court. The latter would refuse to trade unless it was done under its own conditions, namely the appearance of the offering of gifts as a sign of submission and admiration on the part of the distant monarch. In each case, the full equivalent was paid for these offerings in the shape of counter-gifts presented to the so-called Ambassadors by the Chinese Court. Such "tributary" countries were Arabia, Persia and India. The tribute-bearers were in reality nothing better than private merchants who purchased the counter-gifts of the Court, under the pretext of bringing tribute in the name of some distant monarch. Such relations existed between China and India from the oldest times; they had assumed larger dimensions under the Han Dynasty, when certain nations were compelled by force of arms to send in tribute, while others like the Parthians and Syrians volunteered it as a matter of speculation. The regularity with which these transactions took place led to the creation of court-officers connected with their management. We read in *Sui-shu* that an office called *Ssu-fang-Kuan* was established under the Emperor Yang-ti during the period 605-617 at the Chinese capital for the special purpose of receiving the Ambassadors of the countries in the four directions of the compass, *viz.*, those to the east, principally Japan; in the south, represented by the southern barbarians on the continent, and in Indonesia; in the west represented by the Central Asiatic and trans-Himalayan tribes; and in the north representatives of the *pie-ti*, e.g., the Tartars. For each of these four classes of traffic a special officer was appointed, whose duty it was to superintend "the exchange of produce," besides the duties connected with the reception of the mission.

Of all the ports open to trade during the several periods of Chinese history, Canton, or some locality near Canton, is probably the oldest. Dr. Hirth supposes that the ocean-trade between China and the countries of Western Asia had its terminus in some part of Tongking or Annam on the southern frontier of China and he identifies this port with the Eastern terminus of Roman navigation, Kattigara, supporting the suggestion made by Baron von Richtofen. Prof. Hirth also is inclined to believe that this part of Canton, the cradle of foreign trade, has ever since the 3rd century B.C. been one of the main channels of ocean-commerce. The mention of white pigeons being kept on board the sea-going ships may contain a certain hint as to their nationality; the use of carrier-pigeons, according to some historians, was introduced into China by Western Asiatic traders. Carrier-pigeons are mentioned as a familiar Persian institution by Macandi and during the Mongol rule in Persia important news was entrusted to the flying messengers and these were probably introduced into China by the end of 7th century A.D.

Now, T'ien-du or T'ien-chu is the name by which India was known to the Chinese since the 1st century B.C., when Buddhism was introduced from India to China. But a more ancient Chinese name for India is Shin-du. " This name evidently rendering the Sanskrit Sindhu (river), which was taken for India, appears in the Chinese annals about 120 B.C., after the expedition of General Chang-Kien to Western Asia, who reported on the country of Shin-du from hearsay" (Dr. Bretschneider, *Mediæval Researches*). That there was a brisk transmarine commerce between India and China is amply proved from the following Chinese Texts :*

(i) 'The inhabitants of Tats'in (Syria) traffic by sea with Au-hsi (Parthia) and T'ien-chu (India), the profit of which trade is ten-fold,-"*Hou-han-shu.*" [From this passage, it certainly appears that the people of Tats'in traded by sea with

* Vide G. Hirth, *China and the Roman Orient.*

India and China and that the profit derived from this trade was theirs.]

(ii) 'The inhabitants of Au-hsi (Parthia) and T'ien-chu have trade with China ; its profit is hundred-fold'-"*Chin-shu.*" (written c. 265 A.D.)

(iii) 'As regards Tats'in and T'ien-chu far out on the Western ocean, we have to say that although the envoys of the two Han Dynasties, Chang-Chien and Pan Chlao, have experienced the special difficulties of this road, yet traffic in merchandise has been effected and goods have been sent out to the foreign tribes, the force of winds driving them far away across the waves of the sea'—"*Sung-shu*" (written about 500 A.D.).

(iv) 'In the west of it (T'ien-chu or India), they carry on much trade by sea to "Tats' in" and "Au-hsi," specially in the articles of Tats'in, such as all kinds of precious things, coral, amber, chim-pi (gold jadestone) chu-chi (a kind of pearls) etc., -"*Liang-shu*" (written c. 629 A.D.)

(v) 'The merchants of this country frequently visit Funam (Siam), T'ien-chu, Jih-nan (Annam), Chiao-Chih (Tongking)'-"*Liang-shu.*" (date uncertain)

(vi) 'The country of Tats'in, also called Likan, is on the West of the great sea, west of Au-hsi (Parthia). They always wish to send embassies to China, but the Parthians wanted to make profit out of their trade with us and would not allow us to pass their country. Further, they are always anxious to get Chinese silk'-"*Wei-lio*" (composed in 220-224 A.D.)

(vii) The fleet of one-hundred and twenty-five vessels which sailed from Myos Hormos to the coast of Malabar or Ceylon annually, about the time of the summer solstice, traversed the ocean with the periodical assistance of the monsoon in about 40 days. It appears also from *Wu-shih-wai-kuo-chuan* *i.e.* the account of foreign countries at the time of Wu, 222 A.D. that "ships were provided with seven sails; they sailed from Kang-tiao-chou and with favourable winds could enter Tats'in within a month". Dr. Bretschneider presumed that the city of Kang-tiao-chou was on or near the Indian west-coast. (See his article in the China Review).

Thus the port of Tats'in, at which the Chinese and Indian goods were chiefly landed, must have been at the head of the present Gulf of Akabah, the ancient Sinus Ælanitius (Strabo, XVI, p. 781). The natural advantages of a country like Syria must at any time have commanded a superior position in oriental trade, which is quite compatible with its comparatively inferior position as a political power. Near the port was the city of Petra, so-called by the Greek conquerors. During the first two centuries A.D., Petra was the seat of an immense commerce—the great emporium of Indian commodities, where merchants from all parts of the globe, met for the purposes of traffic.* The city fell under the Muhammedan Empire and from

* Kiepert, *Lehrb. d. alten Geogr.* p. 184.

that time to the beginning of the present century was nearly lost to the memory of man. When the celebrated Swiss traveller Burckhardt discovered its forgotten site in 1811, he found only a solitary column and one ruined edifice left standing of all the sumptuous structures that once crowded this romantic vale. It need hardly be added that the prosperity of Petra was mainly dependent upon the caravan-trade, which at this entrepôt changed carriage and passed from the hands of the southern to the northern merchants. Mommsen writes that "it was in the ports of the Nabatæan merchants, in the peninsula of Sinai and in the neighbourhood of Petra, that goods coming from the Mediterranean were exchanged for Indian produce."

The introduction of Buddhism from India was an event of the highest importance for the moral development of China and is the most striking incident of the rule of Han Dynasty and indeed in the whole of China's history. An unauthenticated account states that Indian missionaries had entered China as early as 227 B.C. and in 122 B.C. a Chinese expedition is said to have advanced beyond Yarkand and to have brought back a golden image of Buddha. Communication between India and China becomes very frequent from this date. Knowledge of foreign doctrine entered the country and in 61 A.D. Emperor Ming-ti sent messengers to India to bring back Buddhist books and priests. The priests were brought and one of them Kashiapmadanga (Kāsyapa Mātanga) translated a Sutta in Layong. He is followed in the same year by Fa-lan, like the other, a Sramana of Central India.

The development of Buddhism seems to have advanced somewhat slowly at first. Not until the beginning of the 4th century do we hear men of Chinese rank began to take upon themselves the vows of Buddhist monks. At the same period large monasteries were erected in North China and nine-tenths of the common people are said at that time to have embraced the Buddhist teaching. The kingdom of Tsin seems to have been the chief centre of Buddhism and here in 405, a new translation of the sacred Buddhist books was brought out. An army was sent to India and brought back teachers to Chang-an, who there undertook the work aided by 800 other priests and under the Emperor's personal supervision. Intercourse between China and India being constant at the date, numerous travellers went southward, returned with sages and books and wrote the story of their travels. In 420, the Tsin Dynasty fell and was replaced in the north by the Tartar Wē and in the south by the native dynasty of Sung. The princes of the two new dynasties at first displayed an aversion to Buddhism. But after the death of the first Emperor of the Wē dynasty, permission was given to erect a Buddhist shrine in every town. Similarly the persecution by the Sung princes soon ceased and their government gained a reputation for the special favour which it showed to Buddhism. Embassies arrived from Ceylon and from Kapilavastu, all of which referred to the uniformity of religion, and sang the praises of the Sung Emperors of the kingdom of Yauchen. In 526, the 28th Buddhist patriarch Ta Mo (Bodhidharma) came to China by sea; the downfall of Buddhism in the country of its origin had forced him and many of his co-religionists to seek a new home in China, chiefly in Layong, where 3000 Indians are said to have lived in the 6th century A.D. But in 714, a violent persecution of the Buddhists broke out. In spite of this, however, individual priests continued to occupy state offices and the Indians were entrusted with the arrangements of the Calendar. Under the succeeding dynasties a reaction set in and a strong support was given to Buddhism by the Mongol Dynasty (1280-1388). The semi-barbarous conqueror, Kublai Khan, was a zealous Buddhist and his successors followed his example. Intercourse with India increased and Indian Buddhism began to exercise an important influence on Chinese belief.*

FURTHER INDIA

The prehistoric period of Further India is shrouded in gloom, though a few vague and general indications may be derived from the sciences of comparative philology and anthropology. These indications alike point to early racial commixture and fusion. From a philological point of view, several primordial groups stand out in isolation. We have no means of deciding where the first ancestors of these groups may have dwelt. Upon the dates and histories again of the ancient racial movements we have no information whatever. Chinese histories refer indeed to an Embassy sent from Indo-China probably from Tongking in the year 1110 B.C. to the Imperial Chinese

* Vide Max Von Brandt in "*The World's History.*" Vol. III.

Court of Chau. In 214 B.C. and in 109 A.D. Chinese Generals founded dynasties of their own in Tong-king. However we have no other information upon the general history of those ages. The wild imagination of the natives has so transformed the legends, that though these go back to the creation of the world, they give us no historical material of any value whatsoever.

It is not till the first century A.D. that the general darkness is somewhat lifted. On the northern frontier and in the east, we find a restless movement and a process of struggle with varying success, between the Chinese and the native races, while in the south Hindu civilisation is everywhere victorious. The most important source of our knowledge upon the affairs of Further India in those ages is Ptolemy's description of the world, dating from the first half of the second century A.D. The explanation of many of his statements is due to the energy of Col. Gerini. Ptolemy informs us that in his time the coast-line of Further India was inhabited throughout its length by the Sindoi (Hindus). As their importance in Indo-China was at that time great enough for the Alexandrine geographer to describe as a race of wide distribution, the advance of Hindu civilisation must have taken place at least some centuries previously.

But the introduction of Brahman civilisation was merely a victory for a few representatives of a higher culture. The physical characteristics of the population of Further India were but little influenced by this new infusion. The movement can hardly have begun before the period at which the Brahmans colonised Orissa. From this point Brahmanism apparently made its way to Indo-China by sea. On the one hand, Brahmans did not advance along the land-route, long hidden and leading through the Ganges Delta and Assam, until the second half of the present millennium. On the other hand, the proof of the fact that the colonisation was of a trans-marine origin is the predominance of Hinduism upon the coast (cp. the statement of Ptolemy, above). The movement to Indo-China cannot have started from Southern India, for the reason that Brahmanism at the period had taken but little hold on the south, and the transmission of civilisation from these shores is therefore extremely improbable. It was not until a much later period that the communication between the two countries began, the results of which are apparent in the Dravidian influences visible in the later temple-buildings of Indo-China. Further evidences of the northern origin of Indo-Chinese Brahmanism are the names of more important towns of early Indonesia. which are almost entirely borrowed from Sanskrit names of the towns in the valley of the Ganges, and also the desire of the Indo-Chinese rulers to retrace their origin to the mythical Sun and Moon dynasties of Madhya-desa.

The maritime route led straight to Burmah, but the Indian civilisation at the moment found that province less favourable to its development than that of the great and more hospitable Champa Kingdom in the Central South. The Gulf of Ligor and the banks of the great rivers of Cambodia seem to have been the central points of Brahmanical influence. From Upper Burmah to Cochin-China countless temple-ruins are to be found at the present day, with rich ornamental sculptures and Sanskrit inscriptions, bearing evidence to the force of the Brahmanical influences in earlier ages. Every year important discoveries are made—thanks to ceaseless activity of the archæologists deputed by the French Government. According to M. E. Aymonier, most of the traditional names of the kings of Cambodia are to be read in inscriptions in the Sanskrit form from the 3rd century A.D. to 1108. At a later period, within this district, Sanskrit writing gave place to the native Khemer Script. Inscribed memorials, carvings and buildings generally, make it clear that Siva and his son Ganesa, were the most widely distributed among the Hindu Pantheon. The images and symbols of these gods are far more numerous than those of the other figures of the Hindu Mythology. However, Vishnu at this time was also highly venerated. The most important and beautiful Brahmana temples of Further India are dedicated to this god, instances being the magnificent temples of Angkor Thom and Angkor Vat, built as we learn from the evidence of inscriptions, in 825 A.D. Thus the Hindu immigrants brought with them the gods of Brahmanism and the beautiful legends of the Ramayana. Nowhere do we find any sublime creations equalling in grandeur and artistic perfection those of Angkor Thom and Angkor Vat, which are not only unique in Indo-China or even Asia, but perhaps in the whole world. The bas-relief of Angkor Vat, which stretches its medley of personages for more than a thousand yards on the four sides of the main Temple is inspired by the Ramayana and is evidently carved under Hindu influence. Says M. Pierre Loti in his fascinating volume on "Siam": "This temple is one of the places in the world, where men have heaped together the greatest mass of stones, where they have accumulated the greatest wealth of sculptures, of ornaments, of foliage, of flowers and faces. It is not simple as are the lines of Thebes and Baalbeck. Its complexity is as bewildering even as its enormity. Monsters guard all the flights of steps, all the entrances; the divine Apsarās in indefinitely repeated groups are revealed everywhere amongst the overhanging creepers."

Some centuries later, the powerful sovereigns of Angkor saw arriving from the east, missionaries in yellow robes, bearers of the new light at which the Asiatic world was wondering. Buddha had achieved the enlightenment of India and his emissaries were spreading over the east of Asia, to preach there the same gospel of piety and love, which the disciples of Christ had brought to Europe at a latter period. The temples of Brahma became Buddhist Vihāras; the statues changed their attitudes and lowered their eyes with gentler smiles. Buddhism advanced to Indo-China by two routes. The first of these led straight from India and Ceylon to the opposite coast. According to a tradition, Buddhaghosha in the 5th century A.D., after making the translation of the sacred Scriptures in Pali, introduced the doctrine of Buddha into the country, starting from the island of Ceylon. Resemblances between the script of Cambodia and the Pali of Ceylon testify to the contact of civilisation and religion between these two countries. Subsequently, however, the Northern or Sanskrit developments of Buddhism had advanced to Further India by way of Central and Eastern Asia. The doctrine in this form was first transmitted to the vigorous and semi-barbaric tribes of the mountainous highlands, who seemed to have accepted it readily. At any rate, the Thai races (Laos, Shans and Siamese) who migrated southward at a later period were undoubtedly zealous Buddhists. Their advance about the end of the first and second centuries A.D. implies a definite retrogression on the part of Brahmanism in Indo-China. Brahmanism decayed and the temples sank into ruin. Upon their sites arose buildings, which in the poverty of decoration and artistic conception correspond to the humility of Buddhist theology and metaphysics (see the sculptured figures of Buddha and his Disciples in the interior of the Siamese Pagoda, Vat Sut Hat, in Lucien Fournereau's "*Le Siam Ancien,*" in the *Annals du Musée Guimet*). In Cambodia alone did Brahmanism maintain its position for a time, as is evidenced by the buildings and inscriptions from the 6th to the 18th centuries. About the year 700, the northern type of Buddhism made an unobtrusive entrance and King Jayavarman (968-1002) undertook reforms on behalf of Buddhism.

Brahmanism had been however very deeply rooted, as is proved by the numerous Sanskrit words borrowed by the modern language of Indo-China and also by many special practices, which have persisted even to the present day. Vishnu, Siva and Ganesa, though no longer worshipped as gods, were honoured as heroes, and their images in bronze and stone decorate the temples side by side with the images of Buddha, as for instance, in the temple of

Vat Bot Phram at Bangkok. Vishnu remains one of the heraldic devices on the royal banner of Siam and the kings of this empire show special favour to the Brahmans in their districts, who cling to the old beliefs. The aristocracy of Cambodia too still lays claim to certain privileges of the Kshattriyas, which reminds us of the Brahmanical caste-system. The religion of Champâ again was chiefly Siva worship (Lingapujâ) and scarcely a trace of Buddhism is to be discovered during the period from the 3rd to the 11th century. The history of this swift and mysterious decline has never been written and the invading forests guard the secret of it.

INDONESIA.

The Historical Importance of the Indian Ocean.

Of all parts of the mighty ocean which encircles the earth, none next to the Mediterranean seems by its position and shape more adapted to play a part in the history of the world than the Indian Ocean. Just as the Mediterranean basin, so important for the course of history of the human race, parts the immense mass of the old world of the West and breaks it up into numerous sections, so the Indian Ocean penetrates the same land-mass from the South in the shape of an incomparably vaster and crescent-like Gulf, having the continents of Africa and Australia on either side, while directly opposite its northern extremity, lies the giant Asia. In the number, therefore, of the continents surrounding it, the Indian Ocean is inferior to none of the larger sea-basins—neither to its great companion oceans, the Atlantic and the Pacific in the West and the East, nor to the diminutive Mediterranean in the North; each of them is bounded by three continents.

From the historical standpoint the Indian Ocean takes a very high place. It is true that its historical importance is in no way equal to that of the Mediterranean, though the latter is tiny in comparison; but it lies exactly in the latitude, where "the zone of greatest historical density" begins, being closed towards the north by the mighty barrier of the Asiatic continent, and therefore taking a share in that vast trans-oceanic international commerce from the very earliest times. This Ocean, lying as it does on the southern edge of the old world, penetrating at so many points the lands of ancient history and offering such facilities for international intercourse, has been the theatre of events, which are not wanting in grandeur and are sometimes eminently suggestive.

But the remote past of the Indian Ocean is wrapped in the same obscurity as that of the most parts of the earth's surface. We are tempted to dwell on the enigma in this case, because more than one investigator has been inclined to look for the earliest home of the primitive man in one part or another of the Indian Ocean. But it is idle to speculate when we have no sufficient materials for a conclusion. The history of this ocean however is predominantly economic and there is no reason to doubt that if we could penetrate the darkness of the prehistoric past, we should find a radically different state of things. What life and movement there has been on the high ways of the Indian Ocean is mainly due to commerce. Its activity in this sphere is the characteristic feature of its historical aspect; many features of it may have been changed as millennium after millennium rolled on, but the general expression remains the same. All the nations, which ventured out on to the Indian Ocean, especially the Hindus, were chiefly induced to make such voyages for commercial objects. The historical rôle of the Indian Ocean, must therefore be regarded predominantly from the standpoint of the history of trade. In reality, it discloses prospects of remarkable depth and reveals glimpses of the rise and fall of nations, and here also the history of its trade is in fact the history of the civilisation of our race, and, though it is not any longer the only avenue of international commerce, yet its busy waters even now, when the East has been opened up to the widest extent, are the great link of communication between the East and the West.*

The commerce of the Indian Ocean goes back far into remote antiquity. As we have noticed elsewhere, the ancient Egyptians and the Phœnicians were certainly the earliest authenticated navigators of the Indian Ocean and its adjoining parts. Although the ancient Egyptians had an invincible predilection for seclusion, yet they tried at the most different periods to bring themselves into direct communication with the countries producing the spices which they used so much and prized so highly. But the first attempts at direct maritime communication with India from the West were certainly made by the Phœnicians. Even if we put aside the accounts given by Strabo of their early settlements on the Persian Gulf and of their emporia at Tylos

* Vide Dr. K. Weule's article in Helmolt's *Weltgeschichte*, Band III.

and Arados, yet their trading voyages on the north-western Indian Ocean go back to the second millennium B.C. Even at the time of the expedition sent by Hiram of Tyre and Solomon, the magnificent and wise king of the Hebrews, to Ophir from Ezion-geber and Elath, the route to that mysterious land of gold was well-known and regularly frequented. The ease with which they had acquired the monopoly of the Mediterranean must have encouraged the Phœnicians to gain a firm footing on the other expanse of the sea lying within the sphere of their power, especially since this new field for action, with its fabulous treasures which were eagerly coveted by the civilised world of that time, promised advantages such as the Mediterranean, long since navigated by them, could hardly afford.

The magnet however, which chiefly attracted navigators into this ocean was the peninsula of India. India and the Indian Ocean are two inseparable ideas, as is shown by the two names. And yet this close relationship holds good only in a limited sense. The peninsula to the south of the Himalayas is, by its geographical position, fitted to rule the surrounding seas more than any other country which bounds the Indian Ocean. Nevertheless during the long course of its history, it never attained a commanding position. "The fault," asserts Dr. Karl Weule, "lies simply and solely in the ethnographical conditions of India. The Aryans on their descent from the highlands of Iran into the sultry plains of Hindustan were forced to take over another nature and fell victims to it. While adapting themselves in course of time to the new conditions, they paid the natural tribute to the tropical and subtropical climates; they underwent an inner development which culminated in a religious expansion, and never felt the necessity of employing against the outside world the power of their overwhelming numbers and their superior intellectual endowments. The fact that the Vedic hymns and Manu's Code mention Aryan voyages, which extended even to the ancient island of Dioscorides (Socotra) is again and again brought forward as a proof that trade communications existed between India and the West. The Indian Aryans never made a permanent habit of navigation. India never felt the need of seeking the outside world, but it always was destined to be the goal for the other nations, by land as well as by sea. From its vast treasures it has given to the world more than any other country on the earth, but the world has had to fetch these treasures for itself." We must admit that Dr. Weule's statement is true only in a qualified sense, for the Indian civilisation profoundly impressed the culture of the Indonesians, the Siamese and even the Cambodians from very early times, and the ancient Hindus were not wholly averse to navigation.

The influences of the voyages and settlements of the Aryan Hindus were not so powerful as those foreign forces which were continually at work owing to the favourable position of the islands of the Malaya Archipelago, for purposes of intercourse. Asiatic nations had long sought out the Archipelago, had founded settlements and had been occasionally compelled to exercise some political influence. The islands were indeed not only the half-way houses for communication between Eastern Asia and the West, but they themselves offered coveted treasures. First and foremost among these were spices, the staple of the Indian trade; gold and diamonds were found in the mines of Borneo and there were many other valuable products. The Chinese from East Asia obtained a footing in the Malaya Archipelago; from the West came the agents of the Indonesian and East Asiatic commerce—the Hindus first, then the Arabs, and soon after them the first Europeans, the present rulers of the Indonesian island-world.

But the inhabitants of India influenced their insular neighbours quite differently from the Chinese. They brought to them, together with an advanced civilisation, a new religion, or rather two religions, which were destined to strike root side by side in the Archipelago—Brahmanism and Buddhism. Probably the first to cross the Bay of Bengal were the sea-loving inhabitants of the Sunda Islands themselves, who as bold pirates, like the Norwegian Vikings, ravaged the coasts but also sowed the first seeds of commerce. After this, the inhabitants of the coasts of Nearer India, who had hitherto kept a brisk intercourse only with Arabia and the Persian Gulf, found something very attractive in the intercourse with Indonesia, which induced some enterprising merchants to sail to the islands so rich in spices, until at last an organised and profitable trade was opened. Many centuries however must needs elapse before the spiritual influence of the Indian culture really made itself felt there.

Since the Hindu has as little taste for recording history as the Malay, the beginning of the intercourse between two groups of peoples can only be settled by indirect evidence. John Crawfurd in this connection relies on the fact that the two articles of trade peculiar to Indonesia, and in earlier times procurable from no other source, were the cloves and the nutmegs. The first appearance of these products on the Western markets must accordingly give an indication of the latest date at which the intercourse of Nearer India with the Malaya Archipelago can have been systematically developed. Both these spices were named among the spices imported to Alexandria for the first time in the age of Marcus Aurelius, i. e., 180 A.D., while a century earlier "The Periplus of the Erythræan Sea" does not mention them. If then we reflect that a certain time would have been required to familiarise the natives of India with these spices, before there was any idea of shipping them further, and that perhaps on the first trading voyages, which must necessarily have been directed towards the Straits of Malacca, products of that region first and then the spices, which grow in the more distant parts of the Archipelago, had been exchanged, we are justified in placing the Indian-Malaya trade in the first century of the Christian era. Chinese accounts lead us to suppose that at this time Indian merchants had even reached the south-east of China. At a later period, more detailed accounts of Indonesia reached the Græco-Roman World. Even before cloves and nutmegs appeared in the trade-lists of Alexandria, Ptolemy the geographer had already inserted on his Map of the World the names "Malayu" and "Jawa." Various other facts point to the position of Java as the centre of the civilisation of Indonesia, and as the emporium for the commerce which, some centuries later, was destined to allure even the ponderous junks of the Chinese to a voyage along its coast.

Following in the tracks of the merchants and perhaps themselves condescending to do a stroke of business, Indian priests gradually came to the islands and won reputation and importance there. India itself, however, at the beginning of the Christian era was not a united country from the religious point of view. Buddhism like an invading torrent, had destroyed the old Brahma Creed, had shattered the caste-system and had then sent out its missionaries to achieve splendid success in almost all the surrounding countries. But it had not been able to destroy altogether the old religion of the land; Brahmanism once more asserted itself with an inexhaustible vitality. The growth of the Hindu influence on Indonesia falls in this transition period, when the two forms of religion existed side by side and the religious disputes in India are not without importance for this outpost of Indian culture. Buddhists and Brahmans came on the scene, side by side, often avowedly as rivals, although it remains doubtful whether the schism led to warlike complications. The fortunes of the two sects in the Malaya Archipelago are remarkably like those of their co-religionists in India. In the former region, Buddhism was temporarily victorious, and left its marks on the most glorious epoch of Javanese history; but Brahmanism showed greater vitality and has not yet been entirely rooted out while the Buddhist faith only speaks to us from the gigantic ruins of the temples.

The thought is suggested that the Brahmanical Hindus came from a different part of the peninsula to the Buddhist. Dr. Fergusson conjectured the home of the Buddhist immigrants to be at Gujrat and at the mouths of the Kistna. The architecture of the Buddhist temples in Java and the language of the Sanskrit inscriptions found there lend colour to this view. We may mention, however, that recently it has been suggested by Dr. H. Kern and Dr. J. Groneman, the great authorities on Buddhism, that the celebrated temples of Boro-Budur must have been erected between 850 and 900 A.D. by the followers of the Southern Buddhists (Hinayanists), whose sects, for example, predominated on Southern Sumatra in the kingdom of Sri-Bhoja. Brahmanical and Buddhist monuments did not appear simultaneously in Java. The most ancient temples were certainly erected not by the Buddhists but by the worshippers of Vishnu in the 5th century A.D. Some inscriptions found in the west Java, which may also be ascribed to the followers of Vishnu date from the same century. The Chinese Buddhist, Fa Hian, who visited the island about this time mentions the Hindus, but does not appear to have found any members of his own faith there. According to this view, the Indians of the Coromondel Coast would have first established commercial relations with Indonesia, and it was only at a later period that they were followed by the inhabitants of the north-west coast of India. These also being connected with the civilised countries of the West, gave a great stimulus to trade and became the leading spirits of the Indian colony in Java. This explains then the later predominance of Buddhism in the Malaya Archipelago.*

In the eighth century A.D., the immigration of the Hindus, including in their number many Buddhists, seems to have increased in Java to an extraordinary extent; the construction of a Buddhist temple at Kalasan in the year 779 A.D. is recorded in inscriptions. The victory of Indian civilisation was confirmed and the rulers turned with enthusiasm to the new forms of belief, and spent their accumulated riches in the erection of gigantic temples modelled upon those of India. From Java, which was then the political centre of the Archipelago, the culture and religion of the Hindus spread to the neighbouring islands, to Sumatra, South Borneo, and other parts of the Archipelago. The most easterly points where Buddhism achieved any results were the island of Ternate and the islet of Tobi, north-east of Halmahera, which already formed a stepping-stone to Micronesia. At that time Pali was the language of the educated classes. The Indian system of writing stimulated the creation of the native scripts, even among those tribes, which, like the Battaks in the interior of Sumatra, were but slightly affected in other respects by the wake of Indian civilisation. The influence of India subsequently diminished. In the 15th century it once more revived, a fact that may certainly be connected with the political condition of Java. Since Buddhism had at this time almost disappeared in Nearer India, this revival also implies a strengthening of the Brahmanical doctrines, which had survived therefore

---

* Vide Dr. Heinrich Schurtz in the *History of the World* Vol. II

the fall of Indian civilisation in the Malaya Archipelago.

Now let us examine the extent of the influence of the Indian culture on some of the important islands of the Archipelago in detail.

JAVA

No reliable history of the island is forthcoming, since the first records, which are still untrustworthy, date from the Islamic age. We are thus compelled to have recourse to the accounts supplied by other nations, and to the remains of buildings, which are still to be found plentifully on the island. In any case, Java seems to have been the focus of the Archipelago,so far as civilisation was concerned, and to some extent the political centre also, and it has retained this position down to the present day. Our oldest information about Java can be traced to the Indian traders, who had communications with the island since perhaps the beginning of the Christian era. But according to a prophetic chronology of the Javanese, which is now in the possession of the Susuhunan and is ascribed to the pen of Aji Jaya Baya, the supposed arrival of Aji Saka did not take place till after the year 1000. "What was first known of Java," records the Chronicler, "was a range of hills called Gunung Kendong, which extends along the north and south coasts ; it was then that the island first came into notice and at that period commenced the Java era. After this, the Prince of Rom, sent 20,000 families to people Java ; but all of them perished except 20 families who returned to Rom.

In the following year, 20,000 families were sent to Java by the Prince of Kling (India). These people prospered and multiplied. They continued however in an uncivilised state till the year 289, when the Almighty blessed them with a Prince, named Kano."* But in the ancient Hindu chronicles no trace has yet been found of a record of this first expedition from Hindustan to Java.

The fact remains however that the ancient Indians turned special attention to Java which was known to them as Java-Dwipa or *vulgo* "the Island of Barley." This name was given by the first Hindus to both Sumatra and Java, on account of the discovery of this cereal, which according to the tradition they found growing there wild. Java-Dwipa does not however mean the "Island of the Barley," for a very simple reason, and that is that barley will not grow there. The name of the island, it is true, spelt Java in the Sanskrit inscriptions discovered there, but it may be an abridged form of Yavana, that is 'the barbarians.'† But although Java was by no means the nearest island of the Archipelago, the fact that the Hindus first went there, must certainly be due to the existence there of rudimentary political societies whose rulers protected the traders and whose inhabitants had already passed that primitive stage when men have no wants. The Indian merchants by transplanting their culture to Java and giving the princes an opportunity to increase their power and wealth through trade, had no small share in the work of political consolidation. We must treat as a mythical incar-

* Vide Sir S. Raffles' "*History of Java,*" vol. ii, p. 73.

† Vide Col. Gerini, *Researches on Ptolemy's Geography.*

nation of these influences, Aji-Saka, who stands at the beginning of the native tradition. He, like his predecessor Oannes in ancient Babylonia, gave the Javanese their culture and religion, organised their constitution, made laws and introduced the system of writing.

The first immigrants to Java were worshippers of Vishnu, who were followed later by Buddhists; these facts appear from the inscriptions and ruins and are confirmed by the accounts of the Chinese traveller, Fa Hian. The oldest traces of the Hindus have been discovered in West Java, not far from the modern Batavia. There must have been a kingdom in that part between 400 and 500 A.D., whose monarch was already favourable to the new culture and religion. It is possible that the first Buddhists then appeared on the island and acquired influence. Important inscriptions dating from the 7th century tell us of a prince of West Java, Āditya Dharma, an enthusiastic Buddhist and a ruler of a kingdom which comprised parts of the neighbouring Sumatra; he conquered the Javanese prince Siwarāga, whose name leads us to conclude that he was a supporter of the Brahmanical doctrines of Siva and built a magnificent palace in a part of Java, which can no longer be identified. We learn further from the Chinese sources that there was a kingdom of Java, to which 28 petty princes owed allegiance, and that in the year 674 a lady named Sima was on the throne.

Buddhism, supported by a brisk immigration from India increased rapidly in power at this time, especially in the central parts of Java, while in the east and perhaps in the west also, Brahmanism held its own. In the eighth and ninth centuries there were flourishing Buddhist kingdoms, whose power and splendour may be conjectured from the magnificent architectural remains, above all the ruins of temples in the centre of the island, and from numerous inscriptions. If we may judge of the importance of the states by the remains of the temples, the kingdom of Buro-Budur must have surpassed all others. For the greatest of all the temples in Java or even in Asia is that of Boro-Budur.* Buddhism has in fact left no such record anywhere else. In size, it is second in the world only to the great Egyptian Pyramids, but it is first in being far more costly and beautiful. Moreover the amount of human labour expended on the great Pyramids sinks into insignificance when compared to that required to complete this sculptured hill-temple in the interior of Java; and, as the Pyramids surpass the Vihara in height and area and as everlasting monoliths, so do the Boro-Budur surpass the Egyptian monuments in decorative elaboration, in its three miles of alto and bas-reliefs and in its thousands of statues. Indeed its artistic value has no equal.

After the first quarter of the tenth century, hardly any more temples or inscriptions seem to have been erected in Central Java, a significant sign of the complete decay of the national forces. At the same time, the centre of gravity of political power shifted to the east of the island. Inscriptions of the eleventh century tell us of a king Er-langa, who by successful conquests brought a large part of Java under his rule. He was however thoroughly imbued

* Vide Scheltema *Monumental Java*.

with Indian culture, as may be concluded from the increase of Sanskrit inscriptions in the East Java after the beginning of the eleventh century. The next centuries are somewhat obscure, from which may be concluded a certain decline in tràde and in the influence of Indian civilisation. This condition of things lasted until the intercourse with Nearer India once more revived in the kingdoms of Solo and Semarang. This new Hinduistic age in which Brahmanism again became prominent had a stimulating influence on the east of the Island where the kingdom of Modyopahit rose to be a mighty power in 1278 ; in the west, at that time, the kingdom of Pajojaram was the foremost power.

But in spite of all the brilliance of the Hindu States, the seeds of corruption were early sown in them. The immense prosperity of the Javanese people had, early in the ninth century, brought into the country the Arab merchant, who ended in permanently settling there, as the merchants of India had already done, and who won converts for Islam in the different parts of the Archipelago. It was characteristic of this heroic age of Islam that the Arab merchants had other aims beyond winning rich profits from trade ; they tried to obtain political dominion by means of religious proselytism. Apparently the kingdom of Modyopahit, the bulwark of Hinduism, had early been fixed upon as the goal of their efforts. The comparatively feeble resistance of the Buddhistic and Brahmanical doctrines is partly explained by the fact that both were really comprehended by the higher classes alone, while the masses clung to outward forms only. The victory of Islam in Modyopahit soon had its counterpart in the other states of the Island.

SUMATRA

Sumatra, as might be expected from its position, probably came into contact with India and its culture at a somewhat earlier period than Java, since the rich pepper-growing districts on the Straits of Malacca were the first to create a systematic commerce. It is quite in harmony with these conditions that the districts on the northern extremity of modern Achin, were the earliest to show traces of Hindu influence and consequently the beginnings of an organised national life ; thence this influence spread further to the inland region, where signs of it are to be found even at the present day among the Battaks. The older kingdoms of the northern extremity were Poli and Sumatra. In Java, it was the culture and religion of the Hindus, which made themselves chiefly felt, while the political power remained in the hands of the natives. In North Sumatra, on the contrary, the immigrants from India seemed completely to have assumed the lead in the State and to have created a feudal kingdom quite in the Indian style. While the Indian civilisation thus struck root in the north, Southern Sumatra by its geographical position has always been fated to be in some degree dependent on the populous and powerful Java. In 1377, Southern Sumatra was conquered by the Javanese and for a time it belonged to the kings of Modyopahit. Palembang was then colonised by the Javanese immigrants. About the beginning of the sixteenth century, the political supremacy of the Hindus seems to have been broken up and to have given place to Mahommedanism.*

BALI.

Of all the districts of the Malaya Archipelago, the small Sunda Islands play the least conspicuous part in history. Devoid of any political unity they stagnated in their isolation, until foreign immigration introduced a higher type of social unit and small kingdoms sprang into existence here and there along their coasts. Bali affords a solitary exception to the general rule. The island, although profoundly influenced in ancient times by Java, frequently enjoyed political independence. But when the Brahman states of Java increased in strength towards the close of the first millennium of the Christian era, Bali was also a state with Hindu culture. Only recently, a splendid bas-relief has been discovered in the Temple of Kausamba in Kelungkung, in south-east of Bali, depicting scenes from Hindu Mythology. (It is now in the Ethnographical Museum at Berlin). Ugrasena ruled there in 923 and in 1103 another prince Jayapangu is mentioned. Bali later formed a part of the kingdom of Modyopahit. It was impossible for Islam to convert the Balinese, who at the time when they formed a united people actually assumed the aggressive, oppressed the Mohommedan Sassaks on the temporarily conquered Lombok and menaced Sumbawa. Brah-

* Vide Dr. Schurtz in *The World's History* Vol. iii.

manism defied its rival in this case at least, and has lasted in Bali down to the present day.

BORNEO.

Borneo, the largest of the islands of the Malaya Archipelago, has not hitherto in the course of history attained anything like the importance to which its size should entitle it. A glance at the geographical features of this clumsy shaped island, which is surrounded on almost every side by damp unhealthy lowlands, satisfactorily accounts for this destiny. But the south coast of the island was influenced to a remarkable degree by its proximity to Java. We have not only remains of buildings and idols, but also literary evidence to prove that the Hindu kingdom of Java affected both by conquest and by example the adjoining parts of Borneo. Thus a large Javanese immigration was followed by the introduction of Hindu creeds and Hinduism flourished till Mahommedanism struck root in 1600.

Indonesia, therefore, from the first day that the ancient Hindus reached and ventured on its more or less unwelcome shores, down to the present, has played the part of an intermediary from the point of view of anthropology, commerce, religion and more especially of culture. This peculiar property finds its truest expression, so far as the special history of this part of the world is concerned, in the formation of a Hindu-Moslem sphere of civilisation, which embraced the entire north-west of the Indian Ocean, and whose strongest representative we see before us in Islam. The commercial intercourse has never died out, since the time when it was first started; the nations alone who maintained it have changed. The present culture of the Archipelago has grown up under the influence of this constant intercourse; but the oldest conditions, which are so important for the history of mankind, have nowhere been left unimpaired.

CONCLUSION

From the references in indigenous and foreign contemporary literature, it is apparent therefore that India at all times has been famous for its domestic and foreign trade. In the Greek history, we find definite mention of the Indian merchants; in the early days of the Roman Empire, India was a great commercial centre for the merchants of Italy and Egypt, as it was at a much earlier period for all Asiatic races from Phœnicia in the West to China in the East. In more than one epoch, the resources of India, natural and industrial, as well as intellectual, have made the wealth of great empires. Its delicate tissues, its marvellous colours and dyes, its porcelains and pottery, its works on metals and ivory, its spices and precious stones, its dainty essences and perfumes, have not only been the wonder and delight of Europe, but in no slight degree helped in the revival of its art. But its scholars did not travel. Only a great religious and moral inspiration, like Buddhism, could rouse Hindu thought to seek for geographical expansion. Only here and there we find traces of embassies, sent for political objects to the Courts of China and to the Empires of Rome and to the

Monarchies of Egypt. Yet from the time of Alexander downwards the intellectual life of India was profoundly felt throughout the ancient world. Greece, Persia, Egypt and China even, went to sit at the feet of those serene dreamers on the banks of the Indus and the Ganges under the shades of the banyan trees; and there they marvelled at the power of philosophy to achieve ideal virtue. And what treasures of European fable, legend and mythic lore further testify to the indebtedness of Europe to India, in the sphere of imagination and fancy; the Magic Mirror, the Golden Egg, the Purse of Fortunatus, the Cap of Invisibility. *Ex Oriente Lux* !